The Children Act 2004

Fergus Smith

B.Sc.(Hons), M.A., C.Q.S.W., D.M.S., Dip.M

TROWBRIDGE
LEARNING CENTRE

Children Act Enterprises Ltd
Pantiles Langham Road
Robertsbridge
East Sussex TN32 5EP
tel: 01580 880243

www.caeuk.org

© Fergus Smith 2009

British Library Cataloguing in Publication Data
A catalogue record for this book is available from the
British Library

ISBN 978-1-899986-24-8

Designed and typeset by Helen Joubert Design
Printed in the UK by The Lavenham Press

CAE is an independent organisation which publishes
guides to family and criminal law and provides
consultancy, research, training and independent
investigation services to the public, private and voluntary
sectors.

Contents

Part 4: Advisory and Support Services for Family Proceedings

Part 5: Miscellaneous

www.everychildmatters.gov.uk offers guidance and all
publications relevant to achievement of this Act's aims

Introduction

- This guide is designed for use by all those in England and Wales who work with children and their families.

- It offers easy access to, and reinforces understanding of the provisions of the Children Act 2004 and reflects subsequent amendments and other significant developments.

- The Act itself followed publication on 08.09.03 of the government's formal response to the Victoria Climbie Inquiry and its Green Paper 'Every Child Matters'.

- 'Every Child Matters' proposed changes in policy and law to maximise opportunities and minimise risks for all children, focusing services more effectively around their needs and those of their families.

- On 04.03.04 the government published 'Every Child Matters: Next Steps' detailing responses to its Green Paper and describing a wider, non-legislative programme of change to promote the well-being of all children.

- This was followed on 01.12.04 by 'Every Child Matters: Change for Children' (applicable in England) setting out the national framework for local 'change programmes'.

- The overall aim of the Children Act 2004 is to create clearer accountability for children's services, enable more effective joint working and to secure a better focus on safeguarding children.

Key Points

- To provide a voice for children and young people at national level in England, the Act provides for the establishment of a 'Children's Commissioner' whose role is to promote and safeguard the rights and interests of children (and certain groups of vulnerable young adults).

- Part 2 of the Act introduces the principal legislative proposals of the Green Paper i.e. to support better integrated planning, commissioning and delivery of children's services and to provide for clear accountability by introducing:

  - A duty on local authorities to make arrangements through which key agencies co-operate to improve the well-being of children
  - Wider powers to pool budgets to support the above aim
  - A responsibility for key agencies to have regard to the need to safeguard children and promote their welfare in exercising their normal functions
  - Statutory 'Local Safeguarding Children Boards' (LSCBs) to replace the previous non-statutory Area Child Protection Committees (ACPCs)
  - The power to create databases holding basic information on all children
  - A requirement of local authorities in England to put in place a director of children's services (DCS) to be accountable for, as a minimum, the local

authority's education and social services functions insofar as they relate to children

- A requirement to designate a lead member for children's services to mirror the director's responsibility at a local political level
- An integrated inspection framework and the possibility of joint reviews of all children's services in an area

■ Part 3 of the Act introduces similar provisions to Part 2 to be made in Wales, but reflects the different context by introducing:

- A requirement that Welsh authorities identify lead directors and members for children's services for local authorities, local health boards and NHS trusts

■ Part 4 of the Act provides for the devolution of CAFCASS functions in Wales to the Welsh Assembly.

■ Part 5 of the Act makes further provisions to:

- Strengthen the existing notification arrangements for private fostering, with reserve powers to introduce a registration scheme should these not prove effective
- Clarify and simplify the registration of child minders and day care providers
- Provide for the extension of existing intervention powers in relation to education functions to children's social services
- Provide for an extension of inspection powers under s.38 Education Act 1997

- Create a new duty for local authorities to promote the educational achievement of looked after children and an associated power to transmit data relating to individual children in monitoring this
- Place on local authorities a new duty, before determining what (if any) services to provide under s.17 Children Act 1989 for a particular child in need, to ascertain her/his wishes about provision of those services and give due consideration to them
- Allow for payment of fees to adoption review panel members
- Restrict the grounds on which the battery of a child may be justified as reasonable punishment
- Allow for grants to be paid across the range of children, young people and families services
- Remove the power to make a Care Order at lower threshold than would be required under s.31 Children Act 1989, as a sanction for not complying with a Child Safety Order

PART 1

CHILDREN'S COMMISSIONER

Establishment of a Children's Commissioner [s.1]

- S.1(1) provides that there is to be an office of a Children's Commissioner and s.1(2) gives effect to Schedule 1 which sets out:

  - Status and general powers
  - Appointment and tenure of office
  - Remuneration
  - Staff and pensions
  - Funding, accounts and acceptable evidence of documentation duly executed under the seal of the Children's Commissioner
  - Protection from defamation actions
  - 'Regulated position' as per s.36(6) Criminal Justice and Court Services Act 2000
  - Disqualification criteria as per House of Commons Disqualification Act 1975 i.e. the Commissioner and staff cannot be members of the House of Commons

General Function of Children's Commissioner [s.2]

■ The Children's Commissioner has the function of promoting awareness of the views and interests of children in England [s.2 (1)].

■ S/he may in particular, under s.2:

- Encourage persons exercising functions or engaged in activities affecting children to take account of their rights, views and interests
- Advise the Secretary of State on the views and interests of children
- Consider or research the operation of complaints procedures so far as relating to children
- Consider or research any other matter relating to the interests of children
- Publish a report on any matter considered or researched by her/him under s.2 [s.2(2)]

■ The Children's Commissioner is to be concerned in particular under s.2 with the views and interests of children so far as they relate to the following aspects of their well-being:

- Physical and mental health and emotional well-being
- Protection from harm and neglect
- Education, training and recreation
- The contribution made by them to society
- Social and economic well-being [s.2(3)]

■ The Children's Commissioner must take reasonable steps to involve children in the discharge of her/his functions under s.2, in particular to:

- Ensure children are made aware of the function and how they may communicate with her/him
- Consult children and organisations working with children, on the matters s/he proposes to consider or research under s.2(2)(c) or (d) i.e. operation of complaints procedures so far as relating to children or any other matter relating to the health of children [s.2(4)]

■ When the Children's Commissioner publishes a report under s.2, s/he must, if and to the extent s/he considers it appropriate, also publish it in a version suitable for children (or if the report relates to a particular group of children, for those children) [s.2 (5)].

■ The Children's Commissioner must, for the purposes of s.2 (4) have particular regard to groups of children who do not have other adequate means by which they can make their views known [s.2 (6)].

■ The Children's Commissioner is not, under s.2, able to conduct an investigation of the case of an individual child [s.2(7)]

■ The Children's Commissioner or a person authorised by her/him may for the purposes of the s.2 function at any reasonable time:

- Enter any premises, other than a private dwelling, for the purposes of interviewing any child accommodated or cared for there and
- If the child consents, interview her/him in private [s.2(8)]

■ Any person exercising functions under any law must supply the Children's Commissioner with such information s/he has relating to her/his functions as the Commissioner may reasonably request for her/his role under s.2 (provided the information is such that the person, part from s.2 is able to lawfully disclose to her/him) [s.2(9)].

■ When the Children's Commissioner has published a report under s.2 containing recommendations in respect of any person with legal duties/powers, s/he may require that person to state in writing within such a period as the Commissioner may reasonably require, what action the person has taken or proposes to take in response to her/his recommendations [s.2(10]

■ In considering for the purpose of her/his function under s.2 what constitutes the rights and interests of children (generally or so far as relating to a particular matter) the Children's Commissioner must have regard to the United Nations Convention on the Rights of the Child [s.2(11)].

NB. Reference to this Convention in s.2(11) is to the Convention on the Rights of the Child adopted by the General Assembly of the UN on 20.11.89, subject to

*any reservations, objections or interpretative
declarations by the UK for the time being in force
[s.2(12)].*

Inquiries Initiated by Commissioner [s.3]

- When the Children's Commissioner considers that the case of an individual child in England raises issues of public policy of relevance to other children, s/he may hold an inquiry into that case for the purpose of investigating and making recommendations about those issues [s.3(1)].

- The Children's Commissioner may only conduct an inquiry under s.3 if s/he is satisfied that the inquiry would not duplicate work that is the function of another person (having consulted such persons as s/he considers appropriate) [s.3 (2)].

- Before holding an inquiry under s.4 the Children's Commissioner must consult the Secretary of State [s.3 (3)].

- The Commissioner may, if s/he thinks fit, hold an inquiry under s.3, or any part of it, in private [s.3 (4)].

- As soon as possible after completing an inquiry under s.3 the Children's Commissioner must:

  - Publish a report containing her/his recommendations and
  - Send a copy to the Secretary of State [s.3(5)]

- The report need not identify any individual child if the Children's Commissioner considers that it would be undesirable for the identity of the child to be made public [s.3 (6)].

■ When the Children's Commissioner has published a report under s.3 containing recommendations in respect of any person with legal duties/powers, s/he may require that person to state in writing within such a period as the Commissioner may reasonably require, what action the person has taken or proposes to take in response to her/his recommendations [s.3(7)]

NB. S. 250(2) and (3) Local Government Act 1972 apply for the purposes of an inquiry held under s.3 with the substitution for references to the person appointed to hold the inquiry of references to the Children's Commissioner [s.3(8)].

Other Inquiries Held by Commissioner [s.4]

■ When the Secretary of State considers that the case of an individual child in England raises issues of relevance to other children, s/he may direct the Children's Commissioner to hold an inquiry into that case [s.4(1)].

■ The Children's Commissioner may, if s/he thinks fit, hold a s.5 inquiry or any part of it, in private [s.4 (2)].

■ The Children's Commissioner must, as soon as possible after the completion of an inquiry under s.4 make a report in relation to the inquiry and send a copy to the Secretary of State [s.4(3)].

■ The Secretary of State must, subject to s.4 (5), publish each report received by her/him under s.4 [s.4 (4)].

■ When a report made under s.4 identifies an individual child and the Secretary of State considers it would be undesirable for the identity of her/him to be made public:

• The Secretary of State may make such amendments to the report as are necessary to protect the identity of the child and publish the amended report only, or

• If s/he considers that it is not possible to publish the report without identifying the child, s/he need not publish the report [s.4(5)]

■ The Secretary of State must lay a copy of each report published by her/him under s.5 before each House of Parliament [s.4 (6)].

NB. s. 250 (2) to (5) Local Government Act 1972 apply for the purposes of an inquiry held under s.4 in England [s.4(7)] i.e. the Commissioner will be able to summons people to attend to give evidence or to produce documents, to administer oaths and take evidence on oath.

Functions of Commissioner in Wales [s.5]

- The Children's Commissioner has the function of promoting awareness of the views and interests of children in Wales except in so far as relating to any matter falling within the remit of the Children's Commissioner for Wales under s.72B, s.73 or s.74 of the Care Standards Act 2000 [s.5(1)].

  NB. S.72B, s.73 and s.74 above refer to the review of the exercise of functions of the Welsh Assembly and other persons, review and monitoring of complaints arrangements and the examination of individual cases respectively i.e. the role of the Children's Commissioner for Wales.

- S.2 (2) to s.2 (12) describing the general functions of the Children's Commissioner also apply to her/his responsibilities in Wales under s.5 (1) [s.5 (2)].

- In discharging her/his function under s.5(1) the Children's Commissioner must take account of the views of, and any work undertaken by the Children's Commissioner for Wales [s.5(3)].

- When the Children's Commissioner considers that the case of an individual child in Wales raises issues of public policy of relevance to other children, other than issues relating to s.5(1) above, s/he may hold an inquiry into that case for the purpose of investigating and making recommendations about those issues [s.5(4)].

NB. S.3 (2) to s.3 (8) apply to an inquiry held under s.5 (4) above [s.5 (5)].

■ When the Secretary of State considers that the case of an individual child in Wales raises issues of relevance to other children, other than issues relating to a matter referred to in s.5(1), s/he may direct the Children's Commissioner to hold an inquiry [s.5(6)].

NB. S.4 (2) to s.4 (7) apply to an inquiry held under s.5 (6) above [s.5 (7)].

Functions of Commissioner in Scotland [s.6]

- The Children's Commissioner has the function of promoting awareness of the views and interests of children in Scotland in relation to reserved matters [s.6 (1)].

- S.2 (2) to s.2 (12) describing the general functions of the Children's Commissioner also apply to her/his responsibilities in Scotland [s.6 (2)].

- In discharging her/his function under s.6(1) the Children's Commissioner must take account of the views of, and any work undertaken by the Commissioner for Children and Young People in Scotland [s.6(3)].

- When the Children's Commissioner considers that the case of an individual child in Scotland raises issues of public policy of relevance to other children in relation to a reserved matter, s/he may hold an inquiry into that case for the purpose of investigating and making recommendations about those issues [s.6(4)].

NB. S.3 (2) to s.3 (7) apply to an inquiry held under s.6 (4) above [s.6 (5)].

S.210 (3) to (5) Local Government (Scotland) Act 1973 apply for the purposes of an enquiry under s.6 (4) above, with the substitution of references to the Children's Commissioner in place of 'person appointed to hold the inquiry' [s.6 (6)].

■ When the Secretary of State considers that the case of an individual child in Scotland raises issues of relevance to other children in relation to a reserved matter, s/he may direct the Children's Commissioner to hold an inquiry into that case [s.6(7)].

NB. S.4 (2) to s.4 (6) apply to an inquiry held under s.6 (7) above [s.6 (8)].

s.210(3) to (8) Local Government (Scotland) Act 1973 apply for the purposes of an enquiry under s.6(7) above, with the substitution (notwithstanding the provisions of s.53 Scotland Act 1998 – transfers of functions to the Scottish Ministers) of references to the Secretary of State in place of references to the Minister inquiry [s.6(9)].

Functions of Children's Commissioner in Northern Ireland [s.7]

■ The Children's Commissioner has the function of promoting awareness of the views and interests of children in Northern Ireland in relation to excepted matters [s7 (1)].

■ S.2 (2) to s.2 (12) describing the general functions of the Children's Commissioner also apply to her/his responsibilities in Northern Ireland [s.7 (2)].

■ In discharging her/his function under s.6(1) the Children's Commissioner must take account of the views of, and any work undertaken by the Commissioner for Children and Young People for Northern Ireland [s.7(3)].

■ When the Children's Commissioner considers that the case of an individual child in Northern Ireland raises issues of public policy of relevance to other children in relation to an excepted matter, s/he may hold an inquiry into that case for the purpose of investigating and making recommendations about those issues [s.7(4)].

NB. S.3 (2) to s.3 (7) apply to an inquiry held under s.7 (4) above [s.7 (5)].

Para. 2 to 5 Schedule 8 Health and Personal Social Services (Northern Ireland) Order 1972 (S.I.

1972/1265 (N.I.14) apply for the purpose of an inquiry under s.7(4) with the substitution of references to the Children's Commissioner in place of 'person appointed to hold the inquiry' [s.7(6)].

■ When the Secretary of State considers that the case of an individual child in Northern Ireland raises issues of relevance to other children in relation to an excepted matter, s/he may direct the Children's Commissioner to hold an inquiry into that case [s.7(7)].

NB. S.4 (2) to s.4 (6) apply to an inquiry held under s.6 (7) above [s.7 (8)].

Para. 2 to 8 Schedule 8 Health and Personal Social Services (Northern Ireland) Order 1972 (S.I. 1972/1265 (N.I.14) apply for the purpose of an inquiry under s.7(7) with the substitution of references to the Secretary of State for references to the Ministry [s.7(9)].

Annual Reports [s.8]

■ As soon as possible after the end of each financial year the Children's Commissioner must make a report on:

- The way in which s/he has discharged her/his function under Part 1, other than functions of holding inquiries
- What s/he has found in the course of exercising those functions during the year and
- The matters s/he intends to consider or research during the next financial year [s.8(1)]

■ The Children's Commissioner must in particular under s.1 (1)(a) i.e. the way her/his functions have been discharged:

- Include an account of the steps taken by her/ him to involve children in that work [s.8(2)]

■ When the Children's Commissioner makes a s.8 report:

- S/he must send a copy to the Secretary of State
- The Secretary of State must lay a copy before each House of Parliament [s.8(3)]

■ The Children's Commissioner must publish a s.8 report as soon as possible after the Secretary of State has laid it before each House of Parliament [s.8(4)].

■ The Children's Commissioner must also, to the extent that s/he considers appropriate, publish any report made under s.8 in a version suitable for children [s.8 (5)].

Care Leavers and Young Persons with Learning Disabilities [s.9]

■ For the purposes of Part 1 of the Children Act 2004 (except s.2(11) and s.2(12) – references to the UN Convention on Rights of the Child –) any reference to a child includes, in addition to a person aged less than 18, one who is 19 or 20 and who has:

- Been looked after by a local authority at any time after attaining the age of 16 or
- A learning disability [s.9(2)]

NB. For the above purpose, a person is looked after by a local authority if, for purposes of the Children Act 1989 s/he is looked after by a local authority in England and Wales; for purposes of the Children (Scotland) Act 1995 by a local authority in Scotland; for purposes of the Children (Northern Ireland) Order 1995 by an authority in Northern Ireland.

'Learning disability' means a state of arrested or incomplete development of mind which induces significant impairment of intelligence and social functioning [s.9 (3)]

PART 2

CHILDREN'S SERVICES IN ENGLAND

General

Targets for Safeguarding & Promoting the Welfare of Children [s.9A introduced by s.195(1) Apprenticeships, Skills, Children & Learning Act 2009]

■ The Secretary of State may, in accordance with regulations, set safeguarding targets for a children's services authority in England [s.9A(1)].

■ The regulations may, in particular:

- Make provision about matters by reference to which safeguarding targets may, or must, be set
- Make provision about periods to which safeguarding targets may, or must, relate
- Make provision about the procedure for setting safeguarding targets
- Specify requirements with which a children's services authority in England must comply in connection with the setting of safeguarding targets [s.9A(2)]

■ In exercising its functions, a children's services authority in England must act in the manner best calculated to secure any safeguarding targets set under s.9A(so far as relating to the area of the authority) are met [s.9A(3)].

■ 'Safeguarding target', in relation to a children's services authority in England, are targets for safeguarding and promoting the welfare of children in the authority's area [s.9A(4)].

Co-operation to Improve Well-Being [s.10]

■ Each children's services authority in England must make arrangements to promote co-operation between:

- The authority
- Each of the authority's relevant partners and
- Such other persons or bodies as the authority consider appropriate, being persons or bodies of any nature who exercise functions or are engaged in activities in relation to children in the authority's area [s.10(1)]

■ The arrangements are to be made with a view to improving the well-being of children in the authority's area so far as relating to:

- Physical and mental health
- Protection from harm and neglect
- Education, training and recreation
- The contribution made by them to society
- Emotional, social and economic well-being [s.10(2)]

■ In making arrangements under s.10, a children's services authority in England must have regard to the importance of parents and other persons caring for children in improving the well-being of children [s.10(3)].

■ For the purposes of s.10, each of the following is a relevant partner of a children's services authority in England:

- Where the authority is a county council for an area for which there is also a district council, the district council
- The police authority and the chief officer of police for a police area any part of which falls within the area of the children's services authority
- A local probation board for an area any part of which falls within the area of the authority
- A youth offending team (YOT) for an area any part of which falls within the area of the authority
- A Strategic Health Authority and Primary Care Trust for an area any part of which falls within the area of the authority
- A person providing services in pursuance of s.68 Education and Skills Act 2008
- The governing body of a maintained school that is maintained by the authority in its capacity as a local education authority
- The proprietor of a school approved by the Secretary of State under s.342 Education Act 1996 and situated in the authority's area
- The proprietor of a city technology college, city college for the technology of the arts or Academy situated in the authority's area

- The governing body of an institution within the further education sector the main site of which is situated in the authority's area
- The Secretary of State, in relation to the Secretary of State's functions under s.2 Employment and Training Act 1973 [s.10(4) as amended by s.193 Apprenticeships, Skills, Children and Learning Act 2009]

NB. By virtue of Sch.1 para. 3 Education Act 1996, 'Pupil Referral Units – PRUs' – to be re-named 'Short Stay Schools' in 2011, are also now 'relevant partners'.

■ The relevant partners of a children's services authority in England must co-operate with the authority in the making of arrangements under s.10 [s.10 (5)].

■ For the purposes of arrangements under s.10, a relevant person or body may:

- Provide staff, good, services, accommodation or other resources to another relevant person or body
- Make contributions to a fund out of which relevant payments may be made [s.10(5A) inserted by s.193(3) Apprenticeships, Skills, Children and Learning Act 2009]

NB. S.10(4)(g) and s.10(6) & (7) were revoked by Sch.16 Part 5 Apprenticeships, Skills, Children and Learning Act 2009.

■ A children's services authority in England and each of their relevant partners must in exercising their functions under this section have regard to any guidance given to them for the purpose by the Secretary of State [s.10(8)].

NB. The DCSF published in March 2010 'Statutory Guidance on Co-operation Arrangements including the Children's Trust Board and Children and Young People's Plan' ISBN 978-1-84775-693-0.

■ Arrangements under s.10 may include arrangements relating to persons:

- Aged 18 and 19
- Over the age of 19 who are receiving services under ss. 23C to 24D Children Act 1989
- Over the age of 19 but under the age of 25 who have a learning difficulty, within the meaning of s.13 Learning and Skills Act 2000, and are receiving services under that Act [s.10(9)]

■ In deciding for the purposes of the penultimate roundel in s.10(4) above, i.e. location of governing body, the authority and governing body must have regard to any guidance given to them by the Secretary of State [s.10(10) inserted by s.193(5) Apprenticeships, Skills, Children and Learning Act 2009].

■ In s.10 as amended:

- 'Governing body' in relation to an institution within the further education sector, has the meaning given by .90 Further Education Act 1992

- 'Institution within the further education sector' has the meaning given by s.4(3) Education Act 1996
- 'Maintained school' has the meaning given by s.39(1) Education Act 2002
- 'Proprietor' in relation to a city technology college, city college for the technology of the arts, Academy or other school, means the person or body of persons responsible for its management
- 'Relevant payment' in relation to a fund, means a payment in respect of expenditure incurred by a relevant person or body contributing to the fund, in the exercise of its functions
- 'Relevant person or body' means a children's services authority in England or a relevant partner of a children's services authority in England [s.10(11) inserted by 193(5) Apprenticeships, Skills, Children and Learning Act 2009]

Arrangements to Safeguard and Promote Welfare [s.11]

- S.11 applies to each of the following:
  - A children's services authority in England
  - A district council which is not such an authority
  - A Strategic Health Authority
  - A Special Health Authority, so far as exercising functions in relation to England, designated by order by the Secretary of State for the purpose of s.11
  - A Primary Care Trust
  - An NHS trust all or most of whose hospitals, establishments and facilities are situated in England
  - An NHS foundation trust
  - The police authority and chief officer of police for a police area in England
  - The British Transport Police Authority, so far as exercising functions in relation to England
  - A local probation board for an area in England
  - A YOT for an area in England
  - The governor of a prison or secure training centre in England (or, in the case of a contracted out prison or secure training centre, its director)
  - Any person to the extent that s/he is providing services in pursuance of s.74 Education and Skills Act 2008 [s.11(1)]

■ Each person and body to whom s.11 applies must make arrangements for ensuring that:

- Their functions are discharged having regard to the need to safeguard and promote the welfare of children and
- Any services provided by another person pursuant to arrangements made by the person or body in the discharge of their functions are provided having regard to that need [s.11(2)]

NB. S.11(3) states that in the case of a children's services authority in England, the reference in s.11(2) to 'functions of the authority' does not include functions to which s.175 Education Act 2002 applies because that section already places a similar duty on local education authorities, schools and further education authorities.

■ Each person and body, to whom s.11 applies must in discharging their duty under it, have regard to any guidance given to them for the purpose by the Secretary of State [s.11 (4)].

Information Databases [s.12]

- The Secretary of State may, for the purpose of arrangements under s.10 or s.11 above, or under s.175 Education Act 2002:

    - By regulations require children's services authorities in England to establish and operate databases containing information in respect of persons to whom such arrangements relate [s.12(1)(a)]
    - Her/himself establish and operate, or make arrangements for the operation and establishment of, one or more databases containing such information [s.12(1)(b)]

- The Secretary of State may for the purposes of the second of the above roundels, by regulations establish a body corporate to establish and operate one or more databases [s.12(2)].

- A database under s.12 may only include information falling within s.12 (4) below, in relation to a person to whom arrangements specified in s.12 (1) relate [s.12 (3)].

- The information referred to in s.12(3) is information of the following descriptions in relation to a person:

    - Name, address, gender and date of birth
    - A number identifying her/him
    - Name and contact details of any person with parental responsibility for her/him (within the

meaning of s.3 Children Act 1989) or who has care of her/him at any time

- Details of any education being received by her/him (including the name and contact details of any educational institution attended)
- Name and contact details of any person providing primary medical services in relation to her/him under Part 1 National Health Service Act 1977
- Name and contact details of any person providing to her/him services of such description as the Secretary of State may by regulations specify
- Information as to the existence of any cause for concern in relation to her/him
- Information of such other description, not including medical records or other personal records, as the Secretary of State may by regulations specify s.12(4)]

NB. No material relating to case notes or history about a child may be included on the database but the flexibility exists to require the inclusion of further basic data if, for example, there were organisational change.

- The Secretary of State may by regulations make provision in relation to the establishment and operation of any database or databases under s.12 [s.12 (5)].

- Regulations under s.12(5) may in particular make provision:

- As to the information which must or may be contained in any database under s.12, subject to the restrictions of s.12 (3)
- Requiring a person or body specified in s.12(7) to disclose information for inclusion in the database [s.12(6)(b)]
- Permitting a person or body specified in s.12(8) to disclose information for inclusion in the database [s.12(6)(c)]
- Permitting or requiring the disclosure of information included in any such database
- Permitting or requiring any person to be given access to any such database for the purpose of adding or reading information
- As to the conditions on which such access must or may be given
- As to the length of time for which information must or may be retained
- As to procedures for ensuring the accuracy of information included in any such database
- In a case where a database is established by virtue of subsection s.12(1)(b), requiring children's services authorities in England to participate in the operation of the database

■ The persons and bodies referred to in s.12(6)(b) are:

- The persons and bodies specified in s.11(1)
- The Learning and Skills Council for England
- The governing body of a maintained school in England (within the meaning of s.175 Education Act 2002)

- The governing body of an institution in England within the further education sector (within the meaning of that section)
- The proprietor of an independent school in England, within the meaning of the Education Act 1996
- A person or body of such other description as the Secretary of State may by regulations specify

■ The persons and bodies referred to in s.12(6)(c) i.e. permitted to disclose information for inclusion in the database are:

- A person registered in England for child minding or the provision of day care under Part 10A Children Act 1989
- A voluntary organisation exercising functions or engaged in activities in relation to persons to whom arrangements specified in s.12(1) relate
- The Commissioners of Inland Revenue
- A registered social landlord
- A person or body of such other description as the Secretary of State may by regulations specify

■ The Secretary of State may provide information for inclusion in a database under s.12 [s.12 (9)].

■ The provision which may be made under s.12 (6) (e) includes provision for a person of a description specified in the regulations to determine what must or may be done under the regulations.

■ Regulations under s.12 (5) may also provide that anything which may be done under regulations under

s.12 (6) (c) to (e) or s.12 (9) may be done
notwithstanding any rule of common law which
prohibits or restricts the disclosure of information.

■ Any person or body establishing or operating a
database under s.12 must in the establishment or
operation of the database have regard to any
guidance, and comply with any direction, given to
that person or body by the Secretary of State
[s.12(12)]

■ Guidance or directions under s.12(12) may in
particular relate to the:

- Management of a database under s.12
- Technical specifications for any such database
- Security of any such database
- Transfer and comparison of information between
  databases under s.12
- Giving of advice in relation to rights under the
  Data Protection Act 1998

*NB. The Children Act 2004 Information Database
(England) Regulations 2007 SI 2182 set out in detail
how the database (known as ContactPoint) was to
work [see also CAE's Personal Guide to ContactPoint]*

Children's Trust Boards

Establishment of Children's Trust Boards (CTBs) [s.12A introduced by s.194 (2) Apprenticeships, Skills, Children & Learning Act 2009]

■ Arrangements made by a children's services authority in England under s.10 must include arrangements for the establishment of a Children's Trust Board (CTB) for its area [s.12A(1) introduced by s.194(2) Apprenticeships, Skills, Children and Learning Act 2009].

■ A CTB must include a representative of each of the following:

  • The establishing authority
  • Each of the establishing authority's relevant partners (subject to s.12A(4)) [s.12A(2)]

■ A CTB may also include any other persons or bodies that the establishing authority, after consulting each of its relevant partners, think appropriate [s.12A(3)]

■ A CTB need not include any of the establishing authority's relevant partners who are of a description prescribed by regulations made by the Secretary of State [s.12A(4)].

- S.12A(2) does not require a CTB to include a separate representative for each of the persons or bodies mentioned in s.12A(2) [s.12A(5)]

- When 2 or more children's services authorities jointly make arrangements under s.10 for the establishment of a CTB, references in s.12B and s.17 to the area of the authority that established the Board are to be read as references to an area consisting of the combined areas of those authorities [s.12A(6)].

  NB. For the purposes of s.12A and s.12B and s.12C 'the establishing authority', in relation to a CTB, is the children's services authority that establishes the Board and a person or body is a 'relevant partner' of a children's services authority if it is a relevant partner of the authority for the purposes of s.10 [s.12A(7)].

Functions & Procedures of Children's Trust Boards (CTBs) [s.12B]

■ The functions of a CTB are:

- Those conferred by or under s.17 or s.17A (children and young people's plans)
- Any further functions conferred by regulations made by the Secretary of State [s.12B(1) introduced by s.194(2) Apprenticeships, Skills, Children and Learning Act 2009]

■ Regulations under s.12B(1) above may confer a function on a CTB only if the function relates to improving the well-being of children or relevant young persons in the area of the establishing authority [s.12B(2)].

■ In s.12B(2) above, 'well-being' means well-being so far as relating to one or more of the matters specified in s.10(2) [s.12B(3)].

■ A CTB must have regard to any guidance given to it by the Secretary of State in connection with:

- Procedures to be followed by it
- Exercise of its functions [s.12B(4)]

■ In s.12B, 'relevant young persons' means persons, other than children, in relation to whom arrangements under s.10 may be made [s.12B(5)].

Funding of Children's Trust Boards (CTBs) [s.12C]

■ The establishing authority and any of its relevant partners represented on a CTB may make payments towards expenditure incurred by, or for purposes connected with, the Board by:

- Making the payments directly or
- Contributing to a fund out of which the payments may be made [s.12C(1)]

■ The establishing authority and any of their relevant partners represented on a CTB may provide staff, goods, services, accommodation or other resources for purposes connected with the functions of the Board [s.12C(2)].

■ 2 or more CTBs may establish and maintain a pooled fund for the purposes of any of their functions [s.12C(3)]. .

■ A pooled fund is a fund:

- Which is made up of contributions by the Boards concerned, and
- Out of which payments may be made towards expenditure incurred in the discharge of functions of any of the Boards [s.12C(4)]

Supply of Information to Children's Trust Boards (CTBs) [s.12D]

■ A person or body represented on a Children's Trust Board must supply to the Board any information requested by the Board for the purpose of enabling or assisting it to perform its functions [s.12D(1)].

■ Information supplied to a Children's Trust Board under s.12D may be used by the Board only for the purpose of enabling or assisting it to perform its functions [s.12D(2)].

■ Information requested under s.12D(1) must be information that relates to:

  • The person or body to whom the request is made
  • A function of that person or body, or
  • 'A person in respect of whom a function is exercisable by that person or body [s.12D(3)]

Local Safeguarding Children Boards

Establishment of Local Safeguarding Children Boards (LSCBs) [s.13]

- Each children's services authority in England must establish a Local Safeguarding Children Board (LSCB) for its area [s.13 (1)].

- A Board established under s.13 must include such representative or representatives of the authority by which it is established, and each Board partner of that authority as the Secretary of State may by regulations prescribe [s.13(2)].

- For the purposes of s.13 each of the following is a Board partner of a children's services authority in England:

  - If the authority is a county council for an area for which there is also a district council, the district council
  - The chief officer of police for a police area any part of which falls within the area of the authority
  - A local probation board for an area any part of which falls within the area of the authority
  - A YOT for an area any part of which falls within the area of the authority

- A Strategic Health Authority and a Primary Care Trust for an area any part of which falls within the area of the authority
- An NHS trust and an NHS foundation trust all or most of whose hospitals, establishments and facilities are situated in the area of the authority
- A person providing services substitute in pursuance of s.68 Education and Skills Act 2008 in any part of the area of the authority
- CAFCASS
- The governor of any secure training centre in the area of the authority (or, in the case of a contracted out secure training centre, its director)
- The governor of any prison in the area of the authority which ordinarily detains children (or, in the case of a contracted out prison, its director)
- The governing body of a maintained school that is maintained by the authority in its capacity as a local education authority
- The proprietor of a city technology college, city college for the technology of the arts or Academy situated in the authority's area
- The governing body of an institution within the further education sector the main site of which is situated in the authority's area [s.13(3)]

■ A children's services authority in England must take reasonable steps to ensure that the LSCB established by it includes representatives of relevant persons and bodies of such descriptions as may be prescribed by the Secretary of State in regulations [s.13(4)].

NB. The Local Safeguarding Children Board (Amendment) Regulations 2010 SI 2010 622 came into force on 01.04.10 and the additional 'prescribed persons and bodies' who now have to be (in England) members of the LSCB are reflected above in the list of Board partners.

- A LSCB established under s.13 may also include representatives of such other relevant persons or bodies as the authority by which it is established consider, after consulting its Board partners, should be represented on it [s.13(5)].

- A children's services authority in England must take reasonable steps to ensure that the LSCB established by it also includes 2 persons who appear to the authority to be representative of persons living in the authority's area [s.13(5A) inserted by s.196 (1) Apprenticeships, Skills, Children & Learning Act 2009].

- An authority may pay remuneration, allowances and expenses to persons who are included by virtue of s.13(5A) in a LSCB established by it [s.13(5B)].

- For the purposes of s.13 (4) and 13(5), relevant persons and bodies are persons and bodies of any nature exercising functions or engaged in activities relating to children in the area of the authority in question [s.13(6)].

- In the establishment of a LSCB under s.13:

- The authority establishing it must co-operate with each of its Board partners and
- Each Board partner must co-operate with the authority [s.13(7)]

■ 2 or more children's services authorities in England may discharge their respective duties under s.13 (1) by establishing a LSCB for their combined area (and where they do so, any reference in s.13 or ss.14 to 16 to the authority establishing the Board shall be read as a reference to the authorities establishing it [s.13(8)].

Functions and Procedure of LSCBs [s.14]

■ The objective of a LSCB established under s.13 is to:

  • Co-ordinate what is done by each person or body represented on the Board by virtue of s.13(2), (4) or (5) for the purposes of safeguarding and promoting the welfare of children in the area of the authority by which it is established and

  • Ensure the effectiveness of what is done by each such person or body for those purposes [s.14(1) as amended by s.196 Apprenticeships, Skills, Children & Learning Act 2009]

■ A LSCB established under s.13 is to have such functions in relation to its objective as the Secretary of State may by regulations prescribe (which may in particular include functions of review or investigation) [s.14(2)].

■ The Secretary of State may by regulations make provision as to the procedures to be followed by a LSCB established under s.13 [s.14(3)]

Annual Reports [s.14A inserted by Apprenticeships, Skills, Children & Learning Act 2009]

- At least every 12 months, a LSCB established under s.13 must prepare and publish a report about safeguarding and promoting the welfare of children in its local area [s.14A(1)]

- The Board must submit a copy of the report to the local Children's Trust Board [s.14A(2)]

- For the purposes of s.14A, the local area of a LSCB is the area of the children's services authority that established the Board

- The local Children's Trust Board, in relation to a LSCB is the Children's Trust Board established for the local Board's area [s.14A(3)]

Supply of Information Requested by LSCBs in England [s.14B introduced by s.8 Children, Schools & Families Act 2010]

■ If a LSCB established under s.13 requests a person or body to supply information specified in the request to the Board, or another person or body specified in the request, the request must be complied with if the 1st and 2nd conditions are met and either the 3rd or 4th condition is met [s.14B(1)].

■ The 1st condition is that the request is made for the purpose of enabling or assisting the Board to perform its functions [s.14B(2)].

■ The 2nd condition is that the request is made to a person or body whose functions or activities are considered by the Board to be such that the person or body is likely to have information relevant to the exercise of a function by the Board [s.14B(3)].

■ The 3rd condition is that the information relates to:

- The person or body to whom the request is made
- A function or activity of that person or body, or
- A person in respect of whom a function is exercisable, or an activity is engaged in, by that person or body [s.14B(4)]

■ The 4th condition is that the information:

- Is information requested by the Board from a person or body to whom information was supplied in compliance with another request under this section, and
- Is the same as, or is derived from, information so supplied [s.14B(5)]

■ The information may be used by the Board, or other person or body to whom it is supplied under s.14B(1), only for the purpose of enabling or assisting the Board to perform its functions [s.14B(6)].

■ A LSCB must have regard to any guidance given to it by the Secretary of State in connection with the exercise of its functions under s.14B [s.14B (7)].

Funding of LSCBs [s.15]

■ Any person or body specified in s.15 (3) may make payments towards expenditure incurred by, or for purposes connected with an LSCB established under s.13 by:

  • Making the payments directly or
  • Contributing to a fund out of which the payments may be made [s.15(1)]

■ Any person or body specified in s.15 (3) may provide staff, goods, services, accommodation or other resources for purposes connected with a LSCB established under s.13 [s.15(2)].

■ The persons and bodies referred to in s.15 (1) and s.15(2) are:

  • The children's services authority in England by which the Board is established
  • Any person who is a Board partner of the authority under s.13(3)(a) to (h) i.e. all those listed except governors of secure training centres and prisons which detain children
  • In a case where the governor of a secure training centre or prison is a Board partner of the authority, the Secretary of State and
  • In a case where the director of a contracted out secure training centre or prison is a Board partner of the authority, the contractor [s.15(3)]

Review by Chief Inspector of LSCBs' Performance in England [s.15A inserted by s.10 Children, Schools & Families Act 2010]

- The Secretary of State may by regulations make provision for the Chief Inspector to conduct a review of the performance of specified functions by a LSCB established under s.13 [s.15A(1)].

- The regulations may allow or require the Chief Inspector to conduct a review, or may require the Chief Inspector to do so in specified circumstances [s.15A(2)].

- They may in particular make provision:

  - About reports to be made on completion of a review
  - Requiring or facilitating the sharing or production of information for the purposes of a review [s.15A(3)]

- In s.15A 'Chief Inspector' means Her Majesty's Chief Inspector of Education, Children's Services and Skills and 'specified' means specified in regulations under s.15A [s.15A(4)].

LSCBs: Supplementary [s.16]

- The Secretary of State may by regulations make provision as to the functions of children's services authorities in England relating to LSCBs established by them [s.16 (1)].

- A children's services authority in England and each of its Board partners must, in exercising its functions relating to a LSCB, have regard to any guidance given to it for the purpose by the Secretary of State [s.16(2)].

NB. The Local Safeguarding Children Board Regulations 2006 n0.2006/90 now define the way LSCBs are to be run and include child death review and serious case review duties.

Local Authority Administration

Children and Young People's Plan (CYPP) [s.17 as substituted by s.194 (3) Apprenticeships, Skills, Children and Learning Act 2009]

■ The Secretary of State may by regulations require a CTB established by virtue of arrangements under s.10 from time to time to prepare and publish a 'children and young people's plan' [s.17(1) as substituted].

■ A children and young people's plan is a plan setting out the strategy of the persons or bodies represented on the Board for co-operating with each other with a view to improving the well-being of children and relevant young persons in the area of the authority that established the Board [s.17(2) as substituted].

NB. In s.17(2) 'well-being' means well-being so far as relating to the matters specified in s.10(2) [s.17(3) as substituted].

■ Regulations under s.17 may in particular make provision as to:

• The matters to be dealt with in a children and young people's plan
• The period to which a children and young people's plan is to relate

- When and how a children and young people's plan must be published
- Keeping a children and young people's plan under review
- Revising a children and young people's plan
- Consultation to be carried out during preparation or revision of a children and young people's plan.
- Other steps required or permitted to be taken in connection with the preparation or revision of a children and young people's plan [s.17(4) as substituted]

NB. In s.17 'relevant young persons' means persons, other than children, in relation to whom arrangements under s.10 may be made [s.17(5)].

Director of Children's Services (DCS) [s.18 as amended by s.17A(4) Apprenticeships, Skills, Children and Learning Act 2009]

- A children's services authority in England may, and with effect from the appointed day must, appoint an officer for the purposes of:

  - The functions conferred on or exercisable by the authority which are specified in s.18(2) and
  - Such other functions conferred on or exercisable by the authority as may be prescribed by the Secretary of State by regulations [s.18(1)]

- The functions referred to in s.18 (1)(a) i.e. conferred on or exercisable by the authority are:

  - Functions conferred on or exercisable by the authority in its capacity as a local education authority
  - Functions conferred on or exercisable by the authority which are social services functions (within the meaning of the Local Authority Social Services Act 1970 so far as those functions relate to children)
  - Functions conferred on the authority under sections 23C to 24D Children Act 1989 (so far as not falling within the category immediately above

Children and Young People's Plan: Implementation [s.17A as substituted by s.194 (3) Apprenticeships, Skills, Children and Learning Act 2009]

- S.17A applies when a CTB prepares a children and young people's plan in accordance with regulations under s.17 [s.17A(1) as substituted].

- The persons and bodies whose strategy for co-operation is set out in the plan must have regard to the plan in exercising their functions [s.17A (2) as substituted].

- The Board must:

  - Monitor the extent to which the persons and bodies whose strategy for co-operation is set o' in the plan are acting in accordance with the plan

  - Prepare and publish an annual report about extent to which, during the year to which th report relates, those persons and bodies h acted in accordance with the plan [s.17A(substituted]

- The functions conferred on the authority under
  ss. 10–12 and s.12C, s.12D and s.17A of this Act
- Any functions exercisable by the authority under
  s.31 Health Act 1999 on behalf of an NHS body
  (within the meaning of that section), so far as
  those functions relate to children [s.18(2)]

■ The first in the above list – 'functions conferred on or
exercisable by the authority in its capacity as local
education authority' does not include:

- Functions under s.120(3) Education Reform Act
  1988 (functions of LEAs with respect to higher
  and further education)
- Functions under s.85(2) and (3) Further and
  Higher Education Act 1992 (finance and
  government of locally funded further and higher
  education)
- Functions under s.15B Education Act 1996 or
  s.23 Learning and Skills Act 2000 (education for
  persons who have attained the age of 19)
- Functions under s.22 Teaching and Higher
  Education Act 1998 (financial support to
  students)
- Such other functions conferred on or exercisable
  by a children's services authority in England in its
  capacity as a local education authority as the
  Secretary of State may by regulations prescribe
  [s.18(3)]

■ An officer appointed by a children's services authority
in England under s.18 is to be known as its director of
children's services (DCS) [s.18 (4)].

■ The DCS appointed by a children's services authority in England may also have responsibilities relating to such functions conferred on or exercisable by the authority, in addition to those specified in s.18(1), as the authority considers appropriate [s.18(5)].

■ The functions in relation to which a director of children's services may have responsibilities by virtue of s.18 (5) include all those referred to in s.18 (3) [s.18(6)].

■ A children's services authority in England must have regard to any guidance given to it by the Secretary of State for the purposes of s.18 [s.18 (7)].

■ 2 or more children's services authorities in England may for the purposes of this s.18, if they consider that the same person can efficiently discharge for both or all of them, the responsibilities of director of children's services concur in the appointment of a person as director of children's services for both or all of them [s.18(8)].

NB. S.18 (9) gives effect to Sch.2 which introduces amendments to remove the previous duties in England to appoint a director of social services and a chief education officer. These functions are assigned instead to the director of children's services and a director of adult services appointed under s.6 Local Authority Social Services Act as amended.

Lead Member (LM) for Children's Services [s.19]

- A children's services authority in England must, in making arrangements for the discharge of the functions conferred on or exercisable by the authority specified in s.18(1) and such other functions conferred on or exercisable by the authority as the authority considers appropriate

  - Designate one of its members as lead member for children's services [s.19(1)]

- A children's services authority in England must have regard to any guidance given to them by the Secretary of State for the purposes of s.19 (1) [s.19 (2)].

Inspection of children's services

Joint Area Reviews [s.20 as amended by Education & Inspection Act 2006]

■ Any 2 or more of the persons and bodies to which s.20 applies must, at the request of the Secretary of State:

- Conduct, in accordance with a timetable drawn up by them and approved by the Secretary of State, a review of all children's services provided in the area of every children's services authority in England or the areas of such children's services authorities in England as may be specified in the request
- Conduct a review of such children's services provided in the area of such children's services authority in England as may be specified in the request [s.20(1)]

■ Any 2 or more of the persons and bodies to which this section applies may conduct a review of any children's services provided in the area of a particular children's services authority in England [s.20 (2)].

■ The purpose of a review under s.20 is to evaluate the extent to which, taken together, the children's services being reviewed improve the well-being of children and relevant young persons (and in particular to evaluate how these services work together to improve their well-being) [s.20 (3)].

■ The persons and bodies to which s.20 applies are:

- The Chief Inspector of Schools
- The Commission for Healthcare Audit and Inspection
- The Audit Commission for Local Authorities and the National Health Service in England and Wales
- The Chief Inspector of constabulary
- Her Majesty's Chief Inspector of the National Probation Service for England and Wales
- Her Majesty's Chief Inspector of Court Administration
- The Chief Inspector of Prisons [s.20(4) as amended]

■ Reviews under s.20 are to be conducted in accordance with arrangements made by the Chief Inspector of Schools [s.20 (5)].

■ Before making arrangements for the purposes of reviews under s.20 the Chief Inspector of Schools must consult such of the other persons and bodies to which this section applies as s/he considers appropriate [s.20(6)].

■ The annual report of the Chief Inspector of Schools required by s.2 (7) (a) School Inspections Act 1996 to be made to the Secretary of State must include an account of reviews under this section; and the power conferred by s.2 (7) (b) to make other reports to the Secretary of State includes a power to make reports about such reviews [s.20 (7)].

- The Secretary of State may by regulations make provision for the purposes of reviews under this section and in particular provision:

  - Requiring or facilitating the sharing or production of information for the purposes of a review under s.20 (including provision for the creation of criminal offences)
  - Authorising any person or body conducting a review under this section to enter any premises for the purposes of the review (including provision for the creation of criminal offences)
  - Imposing requirements as to the making of a report on each review under this section
  - For the making by such persons as may be specified in or under the regulations of written statements of proposed action in the light of the report and the period within which any such action must or may be taken
  - For the provision to members of the public of copies of reports and statements made under the paragraphs immediately above (s.20(8) (c) and (d)) and for charging in respect of any such provision
  - For the dis-application, in consequence of a requirement under this section, of any requirement under any other enactment to

conduct an assessment or to do anything in connection with an assessment [s.20(8)]

■ Regulations under s.20 (8) may in particular make provision by applying enactments falling within s.20 (10) with or without modification, for the purposes of reviews under this section [s.20 (9)].

NB. The enactments falling within s.20 (10) are enactments relating to the powers of persons and bodies to which s.20 applies for the purposes of assessments other than reviews under this section [s.20 (10)].

It is anticipated that the Secretary of State will require joint area reviews to begin in September 2005 and cover all area by 2008.

Framework [s.21]

- The Chief Inspector of Schools must devise a Framework for Inspection of Children's Services ('the Framework') [s.21 (1)].

- The Framework must, for the purpose specified in s.21 (3) below set out principles to be applied by any person or body conducting a relevant assessment [s.21(2)].

- The purpose referred to in s.21(2) above is to ensure that relevant assessments properly evaluate and report on the extent to which children's services improve the well-being of children and relevant young persons [s.21(3)].

- The principles in the Framework may:

  - Include principles relating to the organisation of the results of any relevant assessment
  - Make different provision for different cases [s.21(4)]

- For the purposes of s.21(2) to (4) a relevant assessment is an assessment conducted under any enactment in relation to any children's services [s.21(5)].

- When devising the Framework, the Chief Inspector of Schools must consult the other persons and bodies to which s.20 applies [s.21 (6)].

■ The Chief Inspector of Schools must publish the Framework, but before doing so must:

- Consult such persons and bodies, other than those referred to in s.21(6), as s/he thinks fit and
- Obtain the consent of the Secretary of State [s.21(7)]

■ The Chief Inspector of Schools may at any time revise the Framework (and the consultation and consent requirements of s.21 (6) and s.21(7) apply in relation to revisions to the Framework as to the original Framework) [s.21(8)].

Co-operation and Delegation [s.22]

■ Each person or body with functions under any enactment of conducting assessments of children's services must for the purposes of those assessments co-operate with other persons or bodies with such functions [s.22(1)].

■ A person or body with functions under any enactment of conducting assessments of children's services may delegate any of those functions to any other person or body with such functions [s.22 (2)].

Interpretation of ss.20–22 [s.23 as amended by s.194(5) Apprentices, Skills, Children and Learning Act 2009]

- Assessment for the purposes of ss.20–22 includes an inspection, review, investigation or study [s.23 (2)].

- Children's Services in ss.20-s.22 means:
  - Anything done for or in relation to children and relevant young persons (alone or with other persons) in respect of which, apart from s.20, a person or body to which that section applies conducts any kind of assessment, or secures that any kind of assessment is conducted; or which is specified in, or of a description prescribed by, regulations made by the Secretary of State
  - Any function under ss.10 and s.12B to 19
  - Any function conferred on a children's services authority under s.12 [s.23(3)]

- Relevant young persons in s.20-s.22 means persons, other than children, in relation to whom arrangements under s.10 may be made [s.23 (4)].

- 'The Chief Inspector of Schools' in s.20.-s.22 means Her Majesty's Chief Inspector of Schools in England [s.23(5)]

CHILDREN'S SERVICES IN WALES

General

Co-operation to Improve Well-Being in Wales [s.25]

- Each children's services authority in Wales must make arrangements to promote co-operation between the authority, each of the authority's relevant partners and such other persons or bodies as the authority consider appropriate, being persons or bodies of any nature who exercise functions or are engaged in activities in relation to children in the authority's area [s.25(1)].

- The arrangements are to be made with a view to improving the well-being of children in the authority's area so far as relating to:

  - Physical and mental health
  - Protection from harm and neglect
  - Education, training and recreation
  - The contribution made by them to society
  - Social and economic well-being [s.25(2)]

- In making arrangements under s.25 a children's services authority in Wales must have regard to the importance of parents and other persons caring for children in improving the well-being of children [s.25(3)].

■ For the purposes of this section each of the following is the relevant partner of a children's services authority in Wales:

- The police authority and the chief officer of police for a police area any part of which falls within the area of the children's services authority
- A local probation board for an area any part of which falls within the area of the authority
- A youth offending team for an area any part of which falls within the area of the authority
- A Local Health Board for an area any part of which falls within the area of the authority
- An NHS trust providing services in the area of the authority
- The National Council for Education and Training for Wales [s.25(4)]

■ The relevant partners of a children's services authority in Wales must cooperate with the authority in the making of arrangements under s.25 [s.25 (5)].

■ A children's services authority in Wales and any of their relevant partners may for the purposes of arrangements under this section:

- Provide staff, goods, services, accommodation or other resources
- Establish and maintain a pooled fund [s.25(6)]

■ For the purposes of s.25(6) a pooled fund is a fund:

- Which is made up of contributions by the authority and the relevant partner or partners concerned and
- Out of which payments may be made towards expenditure incurred in the discharge of functions of the authority and functions of the relevant partner or partners [s.25(7)]

■ A children's services authority in Wales and each of their relevant partners must in exercising their functions under this section have regard to any guidance given to them for the purpose by the Assembly [s.25(8)].

NB. The Assembly must obtain the consent of the Secretary of State before giving guidance under s.25 (8) at any time after s.25(4) (a) to (c) come into force i.e. those relating to police, probation and YOTs [s.25(9).

Anticipated guidance will make it clear that there is no expectation that Children's Trusts will be established in Wales.

■ Arrangements under s.25 may include arrangements relating to persons:

- Aged 18 and 19
- Over the age of 19 who are receiving services under ss. 23C to 24D Children Act 1989 youth support services (within the meaning of s.123 Learning and Skills Act 2000 [s.25(10)]

Children and Young People's Plans: Wales [s.26]

- The Assembly may be regulations require a children's service authority in Wales from time to time to prepare and publish a plan setting out the authority's strategy for discharging their functions in relation to children and relevant young persons [s.26(1)].

- Regulations under s.26 may in particular make provision as to:

  - Matters to be dealt with in a plan under s.26
  - Period to which a plan under s.26 is to relate
  - When and how a s.26 plan must be published
  - Keeping a s.26 plan under review
  - Consultation to be carried out during preparation of the plan
  - Implementation of a plan under s.26 [s.26(2)]

- The matters for which provision may be made under s.26(2)(a) include in particular the:

  - Arrangements made or to be made under s.25 by a children's service authority in Wales
  - Strategy or proposals in relation to children and relevant young persons of any person or body with whom a children's services authority in Wales makes or proposes to make such arrangements [s.26 (3)]

- Regulations under s.26 may require a children's services authority in Wales to obtain the Assembly's

approval before publishing a plan under s.26 and
may provide that the Assembly may modify a plan
before approving it [s.26(4)]

■ A children's services authority in Wales must have
regard to any guidance given to them by the
Assembly in relation to how they are to discharge
their functions under regulations under s.26
[s.26(5)].

*NB. In s.26, 'relevant young persons' means the
persons, in addition to children, in relation to whom
arrangements under s.25 may be made [s.26 (6).*

Responsibility for Functions under ss.25 & 26 [s.27]

- A children's services authority in Wales must:

  - Appoint an officer, to be known as the lead director for children and young people's services, for the purposes of co-ordinating and overseeing arrangements made under s.25 and s.26 and
  - Designate one of their members, to be known as the lead member for children and young people's services, to have as/her special care the discharge of the authority's functions under those sections [s.27(1)]

- A Local Health Board must:

  - Appoint an officer, to be known as the Board's lead officer for children and young people's services, for the purposes of the Board's functions under s.25 and
  - Designate one of the Board's members who is not an officer as its lead member for children and young people's services to have the discharge of those functions as her/his special care [s.27(2)]

- An NHS trust to which s.25 applies must:

  - Appoint an executive director, to be known as the trust's lead executive director for children and young people's services, for the purposes of the trust's functions under that section; and

- Designate one of the trust's non-executive directors as its lead non-executive director for children and young people's services to have the discharge of those functions as her/his special care [s.27(3)]

■ Each children's services authority in Wales, Local Health Board and NHS trust to which s.25 applies must have regard to any guidance given to them by the Assembly in relation to:

- Their functions under s.27
- The responsibilities of the persons appointed or designated by them under s.27 [s.27(4)]

Arrangements to Safeguard and Promote Welfare: Wales [s.28]

■ This section applies to each of the following:

- A children's services authority in Wales
- A Local Health Board;
- An NHS trust all or most of whose hospitals, establishments and facilities are situated in Wales
- The police authority and chief officer of police for a police area in Wales
- The British Transport Police Authority , so far as exercising functions in relation to Wales
- A local probation board for an area in Wales
- A youth offending team for an area in Wales
- The governor of a prison or secure training centre in Wales (or, in the case of a contracted out prison or secure training centre, its director)
- Any person to the extent that he is providing services pursuant to
- arrangements made by a children's services authority in Wales under s.123(1)(b) Learning and Skills Act 2000 (youth support services) [s.28(1)]

■ Each person and body to whom s.28 applies must make arrangements for ensuring that:

- Their functions are discharged having regard to the need to safeguard and promote the welfare of children and

- Any services provided by another person pursuant to arrangements made by the person or body in the discharge of their functions are provided having regard to that need [s.28(2)]

■ In the case of a children's services authority in Wales, the reference in ss.28(2) to functions of the authority does not include functions to which s.175 Education Act 2002 applies [s.28(3)].

■ The persons and bodies referred to in s.28(1)(a) to (c) and (i) i.e. a CSA in Wales, Local Health Board, NHS Trust and provider of youth services, must in discharging their duty under s.28 have regard to any guidance given to them for the purpose by the Assembly [s.28(4)].

■ The persons and bodies referred to in s.28 (1)(d) to (g) i.e. police, British Transport Police, probation boards and YOTs in Wales, must in discharging their duty under this section have regard to any guidance given to them for the purpose by the Secretary of State after consultation with the Assembly [s.28(5)]

Information Databases: Wales [s.29]

- The Assembly may for the purpose of arrangements under s.25 or s. 28 above or under s.175 Education Act 2002:

  - B regulations require children's services authorities in Wales to establish and operate databases containing information in respect of persons to whom such arrangements relate
  - Itself establish and operate, or make arrangements for the operation and establishment of, one or more databases containing such information [s.29(1)]

- The Assembly may for the purposes of arrangements under s.29 (1)(b) by regulations establish a body corporate to establish and operate one or more databases [s.29(2)].

- A database under s.29 may only include information falling within s.29 (4) in relation to a person to whom arrangements specified in s.29 (1) relate [s.29 (3)].

- The permissible information referred to in s.29(3) is information of the following descriptions in relation to a person:

  - Name, address, gender and date of birth
  - A number identifying her/him
  - Name and contact details of any person with parental responsibility for him (within the

meaning of s.3 Children Act 1989 or who has care of her/him at any time

- Details of any education being received by her/him (including the name and contact details of any educational institution attended)
- Name and contact details of any person providing primary medical services in relation to him under Part 1 of the National Health Service Act 1977
- Name and contact details of any person providing to her/him services of such description as the Assembly may by regulations specify
- Information as to the existence of any cause for concern in relation to her/him
- Information of such other description, not including medical records or other personal records, as the Assembly may by regulations specify [s.29(4)]

■ Regulations under s.29(5) may in particular make provision:

- As to the information which must or may be contained in an database under s.29 (subject to s.29(3))
- Requiring a person or body specified in s.29(7) to disclose information for inclusion in the database
- Permitting a person or body specified in s.29(8) to disclose information for inclusion in the database
- Permitting or requiring the disclosure of information included in any such database

- Permitting or requiring any person to be given access to any such database for the purpose of adding or reading information
- As to the conditions on which such access must or may be given
- As to the length of time for which information must or may be retained
- As to procedures for ensuring the accuracy of information included in any such database
- In a case where a database is established by virtue of s.29 (1)(b), requiring children's services authorities in Wales to participate in the operation of the database [s.29(6)]

■ The persons and bodies referred to in s.29 (6)(b) are:

- The persons and bodies specified in s.28(1)
- The National Council for Education and Training for Wales
- The governing body of a maintained school in Wales (within the meaning of s.175 Education Act 2002
- The governing body of an institution in Wales within the further education sector (within the meaning of that section)
- The proprietor of an independent school in Wales (within the meaning of the Education Act 1996
- A person or body of such other description as the Assembly may by regulations specify [s.29(7)]

■ The persons and bodies referred to in s.29 (6)(c) i.e. those permitted to disclose information for inclusion in the database are:

- A person registered in Wales for child minding or the provision of day care under Part 10A Children Act 1989
- A voluntary organisation exercising functions or engaged in activities in relation to persons to whom arrangements specified in s.29 (1) relate
- The Commissioners of Inland Revenue
- A registered social landlord
- A person or body of such other description as the Assembly may by regulations specify [s.29(8)]

■ The Assembly and the Secretary of State may provide information for inclusion in a database under s.29 [s.29 (9)].

■ The provision which may be made under s.29 (6)(e) includes provision for a person of a description specified in the regulations to determine what must or may be done under the regulations [s.29(10)].

■ Regulations under s.29 (5) may also provide that anything which may be done under regulations under s.29 (6)(c) to (e) or (9) may be done notwithstanding any rule of common law which prohibits or restricts the disclosure of information [s.29(11)].

■ Regulations under s.29 (1)(a) and s.29(5) may only be made with the consent of the Secretary of State [s.29(12)].

■ Any person or body establishing or operating a database under s.29 must, in the establishment or operation of the database, have regard to any guidance, and comply with any direction, given to that person by the Assembly [s.29 (13)].

■ Guidance or directions under s.29 (12) may in particular relate to:

- Management of a database under s.29
- Technical specifications for any such database
- Security of any such database
- Transfer and comparison of information between databases under s.29
- Giving of advice in relation to rights under the Data Protection Act [s.29(14)]

Inspection of Functions under Part 3 [s.30]

■ Chapter 6 of Part 2 of the Health and Social Care (Community Health and Standards) Act 2003 – functions of the Assembly in relation to social services – shall apply as if anything done by a children's services authority in Wales in the exercise of functions to which s.30 applies were a Welsh local authority social services within the meaning of that Part [s.30 (1)].

■ S.30 applies to the following functions of a children's services authority:

  • The authority's functions under s.25 or s.26, except so far as relating to education, training or youth services (within the meaning of s.123 Learning and Skills Act 2000)
  • The authority's functions under s.28
  • Any function conferred on the authority under s.29 [s.30 (2)].

Local Safeguarding Children Boards (LSCBs)

Establishment of LSCBs in Wales [s.31]]

- Each children's services authority in Wales must establish a LSCB for their area [s.31 (1)].

- A LSCB established under s.31 must include such representative or representatives of:

  - The authority by which it is established, and
  - Each Board partner of that authority as the Assembly may by regulations prescribe [s.31(2)]

- For the purposes of s.31 each of the following is a Board partner of a children's services authority in Wales:

  - Chief officer of police for a police area any part of which falls within the area of the authority
  - A local probation board for an area any part of which falls within the area of the authority
  - A YOT for an area any part of which falls within the area of the authority;
  - A Local Health Board for an area any part of which falls within the area of the authority
  - An NHS trust providing services in the area of the authority

- • The governor of any secure training centre within the area of the authority (or, in the case of a contracted out secure training centre, its director)
- • The governor of any prison in the area of the authority which ordinarily detains children (or, in the case of a contracted out prison, its director).

■ Regulations under s.31(2) that make provision in relation to a Board partner referred to in s.31(3) (a) to (c), (f) or (g) i.e. all except those referring to Local Health Board or NHS Trust partners, may only be made with the consent of the Secretary of State [s.31(4)].

■ A CSA in Wales must take reasonable steps to ensure that the LSCB established by them includes representatives of relevant persons and bodies of such descriptions as may be prescribed by the Assembly [s.s.31(5)].

■ A LSCB established under s.31 may also include representatives of such other relevant persons or bodies as the authority by which it is established consider, after consulting Board partners, should be represented on it [s.31(6)].

■ For the purposes of s.31 (5) and (6), relevant persons and bodies are persons and bodies of any nature exercising functions or engaged in activities relating to children in the area of the authority in question [s.31(7)].

■ In the establishment and operation of a LSCB under s.31:

- The authority establishing it must co-operate with each of its Board partners and
- Each Board partner must co-operate with the authority [s.31(8)]

■ 2 or more children's services authorities in Wales may discharge their respective duties under s.31(1) by establishing a LSCB for their combined area (and if they do so, any reference in s.31 and ss.26 to 28 to the authority establishing the Board shall be read as a reference to the authorities establishing it) [s.31(9)].

Functions and Procedures of LSCBs in Wales Part 3 [s.32]

■ The objective of a LSCB established under s.31 is to:

- Co-ordinate what is done by each person or body represented on the Board for the purposes of safeguarding and promoting the welfare of children in the area of the authority by which it is established and
- Ensure the effectiveness of what is done by each such person or body for those purposes [s.32(1)]

■ A LSCB established under s.31 is to have such functions in relation to its objective as the Assembly may by regulations prescribe (which may in particular include functions of review or investigation) [s.32 (2)].

■ The Assembly may by regulations make provision as to the procedures to be followed by a LSCB established under s.31 [s.32 (3)].

Supply of Information Requested by LSCBs in Wales [s.32A introduced by s.9 Children, Schools & Families Act 2010]

- If a LSCB established under s.31 requests a person or body to supply information specified in the request to the Board, or another person or body specified in the request, the request must be complied with if the 1st and 2nd conditions are met and either the 3rd or 4th condition is met [s.32A(1)]

- The 1st condition is that the request is made for the purpose of enabling or assisting the Board to perform its functions [s.32A (2)].

- The 2nd condition is that the request is made to a person or body whose functions or activities are considered by the Board to be such that the person or body is likely to have information relevant to the exercise of a function by the Board [s.32A(3)].

- The 3rd condition is that the information relates to:

  - The person or body to whom the request is made
  - A function or activity of that person or body, or
  - A person in respect of whom a function is exercisable, or an activity is engaged in, by that person or body [s.32A(4)]

- The 4th condition is that the information:

- • Is information requested by the Board from a person or body to whom information was supplied in compliance with another request under s.32A and
- • Is the same as, or is derived from, information so supplied [s.32A(5)]

■ The information may be used by the Board, or other person or body to whom it is supplied under s.32A(1), only for the purpose of enabling or assisting the Board to perform its functions [s.32A(6)].

■ A LSCB must have regard to any guidance given to it by the Welsh Ministers in connection with the exercise of its functions under s.32A [s.32A(7)].

Funding of LSCBs in Wales [s.33]

■ Any person or body specified in s.33(3) may make payments towards expenditure incurred by, or for purposes connected with, a LSCB established under s.31 by:

- Making the payments directly, or
- Contributing to a fund out of which the payments may be made [s.33(1)]

■ Any person or body specified in s.33 (3) may provide staff, goods, services, accommodation or other resources for purposes connected with a LSCB established under s.31 [s.33(2)].

■ The persons and bodies referred to in s.33(1) and s.33(2) are:

- The children's services authority in Wales by which the Board is established
- Any person who is a Board partner of the authority under section s.31(3)(a) to (e)
- In a case where the governor of a secure training centre or prison is a Board partner of the authority, the Secretary of State
- In a case where the director of a contracted out secure training centre or prison is a Board partner of the authority, the contractor [s.33(3)]

LSCBs in Wales: Supplementary [s.34]

- The Assembly may by regulations make provision as to the functions of children's services authorities in Wales relating to LSCBs established by them [s.34 (1)].

- Children's services authorities in Wales and each of their Board partners must, in exercising their functions relating to a Local LSCB have regard to any guidance given to them for the purpose by the Assembly [s.34(2)].

- The Assembly must obtain the consent of the Secretary of State before giving guidance under s.34(2) at any time after the coming into force of any of paras. (a) to (c), (f) or (g) of s.31(3) i.e. all except those referring to Local Health Board or NHS Trust partners [s.34(3)].

PART 4

ADVISORY AND SUPPORT SERVICES FOR FAMILY PROCEEDINGS

CAFCASS Functions in Wales

Functions of the Assembly Relating to Family Proceedings [s.35]

■ In respect of family proceedings in which the welfare of children ordinarily resident in Wales is or may be in question, it is a function of the Assembly to:

- Safeguard and promote the welfare of the children
- Give advice to any court about any application made to it in such proceedings
- Make provision for the children to be represented in such proceedings
- Provide information, advice and other support for the children and their families [s.35(1)]

■ The Assembly must also make provision for the performance of the functions conferred on Welsh family proceedings officers by virtue of any enactment (whether or not they are exercisable for the purposes of s.35(1) [s.35(2)].

■ In s.35 (1), 'family proceedings' has the meaning given by s.12 Criminal Justice and Court Services Act 2000 [s.35 (3)].

■ In Part 4, 'Welsh family proceedings officer' means:

- Any member of the staff of the Assembly appointed to exercise the functions of a Welsh family proceedings officer and
- Any other individual exercising functions of a Welsh family proceedings officer by virtue of s. 36(2) or (4) [s.35 (4)]

Ancillary Powers of the Assembly [s.36]

■ The Assembly may make arrangements with organisations under which the organisations perform the functions of the Assembly under s.35 on its behalf [s.36 (1)].

■ Arrangements under s.36 (1) may provide for the organisations to designate individuals who may perform functions of Welsh family proceedings officers [s.36 (2)].

■ The Assembly may only make an arrangement under s.36(1) if it is of the opinion that:

  • The functions in question will be performed efficiently and to the required standard and
  • The arrangement represents good value for money [s.36(3)]

■ The Assembly may make arrangements with individuals under which they may perform functions of Welsh family proceedings officers [s.36 (4)].

■ The Assembly may make arrangements with an organisation or individual under which staff of the Assembly engaged in the exercise of its functions under s.35 may work for the organisation or individual [s.36 (5)].

■ The Assembly may make arrangements with an organisation or individual under which any services provided by the Assembly's staff to the Assembly in the exercise of its functions under s.35 are also made available to the organisation or individual s.36(6)].

■ The Assembly may charge for anything done under arrangements under s.36 (5) and (6) [s.36 (7)].

■ In this section, references to organisations include public bodies and private or voluntary organisations [s.36 (8)].

Welsh Family Proceedings Officers [s.37]

■ The Assembly may authorise a Welsh family proceedings officer of a description prescribed in regulations made by the Secretary of State, in the exercise of her/his functions to:

- Conduct litigation in relation to any proceedings in any court
- Exercise a right of audience in any proceedings in any court [s.37(1)]

■ A Welsh family proceedings officer exercising a right to conduct litigation by virtue of s.37(1)(a) who would otherwise have such a right by virtue of s.28(2)(a) Courts and Legal Services Act 1990 is to be treated as having acquired that right solely by virtue of this section [s.37(2)].

■ A Welsh family proceedings officer exercising a right of audience by virtue of s.37(1)(b) who would otherwise have such a right by virtue of s.27(2)(a) Courts and Legal Services Act 1990 is to be treated as having acquired that right solely by virtue of this section.

■ A Welsh family proceedings officer may, subject to rules of court, be cross-examined in any proceedings to the same extent as any witness [s.37(4)].

■ A Welsh family proceedings officer may not be cross-examined merely because s/he is exercising a right to conduct litigation or a right of audience granted in accordance with this section [s.37(5)].

NB. In this section, 'right to conduct litigation' and 'right of audience' have the same meanings as in s.119 Courts and Legal Services Act 1990

Protection of Children [s.39]

■ The Protection of Children Act 1999 shall have effect as if the Assembly, in performing its functions under ss. 29 and 30, were a child care organisation within the meaning of that Act [s.39(1)].

■ Arrangements which the Assembly makes with an organisation under s.36(1) must provide that, before selecting an individual to be employed under the arrangements in a child care position, the organisation:

- Must ascertain whether the individual is included in any of the lists mentioned in s.7(1) Protection of Children Act 1999 and
- If s/he is included in any of those lists, must not select her/him for that employment [s.39(2)]

■ Such arrangements must provide that, if at any time the organisation has power to refer an individual who is or has been employed in a child care position under the arrangements to the Secretary of State under s.2 Protection of Children Act 1999 (inclusion in list on reference following disciplinary actions etc), the organisation must so refer him [s.39(3)].

NB. In s.39, 'child care position' and 'employment' have the same meanings as in the 1999 Act.

Advisory and Support Services for Family Proceedings: Supplementary [s.40]

- Schedule 3 (which makes supplementary and consequential provision relating to this Part, including provision relating to functions of Welsh family proceedings officers) has effect [s.40 (1)].

Sharing of Information [s.41]

- The Assembly and CAFCASS may provide any information to each other for the purposes of their respective functions under this Part and Part 4 Criminal Justice and Court Services Act 2000 (CJCSA 2000) [s.41(1)].

- A Welsh family proceedings officer and an officer of the service (within the meaning given by s.11 (3) CJCSA 2000) may provide any information to each other for the purposes of any of their respective functions [s.41 (2)].

Transfers

Transfer of Property from CAFCASS to Assembly [s.42]

- For the purposes of the exercise of functions conferred on the Assembly by or under this Part, the Assembly and the Secretary of State may jointly by order make one or more schemes for the transfer to the Assembly of property, rights and liabilities of CAFCASS [s.42(1)].

- The reference in s.42 (1) to rights and liabilities does not include rights and liabilities under a contract of employment [s. 42(2)].

- A scheme under this section may:
  - Specify the property, rights and liabilities to be transferred by the scheme or
  - Provide for the determination, in accordance with the scheme, of the property, rights and liabilities to be transferred by the scheme [s.42(3)]

- A scheme under s.42 may include provision for the creation of rights, or the imposition of liabilities, in relation to property transferred by the scheme [s.42 (4)].

- A scheme under s.42 has effect in relation to any property, rights and liabilities to which it applies despite any provision (of whatever nature) which would otherwise prevent, penalise or restrict their transfer [s.42(5)].

■ A right of pre-emption or reverter or other similar right does not operate or become exercisable as a result of any transfer under a scheme under s.42; and in the case of such a transfer, any such right has effect as if the Assembly were the same person in law as CAFCASS and as if the transfer had not taken place [s.42 (6)].

■ The Assembly is to pay such compensation as is just to any person in respect of any right which would, apart from s.42 (5) and (6), have operated in favour of, or become exercisable by, that person but which, in consequence of the operation of those subsections, cannot subsequently operate in his favour or become exercisable by her/him [s.42 (7)].

■ A scheme under s.42 may provide for the determination of any disputes as to whether and, if so, how much compensation is payable under s.42 (7) [s.42 (8)].

■ S.42(5) to (8) apply in relation to the creation of rights in relation to property as they apply in relation to a transfer of property [s.42(9)].

■ A certificate issued by the Secretary of State and the Assembly jointly that any property, rights or liabilities have or have not been transferred by a scheme under s.42 is conclusive evidence as to whether they have or have not been so transferred [s.42(10)].

Transfer of Staff from CAFCASS to Assembly [s.43]

■ For the purpose of the exercise of functions conferred on the Assembly by or under this Part, the Assembly and the Secretary of State may jointly by order make one or more schemes for the transfer of employees of CAFCASS to the Assembly [s.43(1)].

■ A scheme under s.43 may apply to any:

- Description of employees of CAFCASS
- Individual employee of CAFCASS [s.43(2)]

■ A contract of employment of an employee transferred under a scheme under s.43:

- Is not terminated by the transfer and
- Has effect from date of transfer under the scheme as if originally made between employee and Assembly [s.43(3)]

■ Where an employee is so transferred:

- All rights, powers, duties and liabilities of CAFCASS under or in connection with the contract of employment are by virtue of s.43(4) transferred to the Assembly on the date of the transfer under the scheme and
- Anything done before that date by or in relation to CAFCASS in respect of that contract or employee is to be treated from that date as

having been done by or in relation to the Assembly [s.43(4)]

NB. S.43 (4) does not prejudice the generality of s.43(3).

- ■ If the employee informs the Assembly or CAFCASS that s/he objects to the transfer:

  - • S.43(3) and (4) do not apply and
  - • Her/his contract of employment is terminated immediately before the date of transfer but the employee is not to be treated, for any reason, as having been dismissed by CAFCASS [s.43(5)]

- ■ S.43 does not prejudice any right of an employee to terminate her/his contract of employment if (apart from the change of employer) a substantial change is made to her/his detriment in his working conditions [s.43(6)].

- ■ A scheme may be made under s.43 only if any requirements about consultation prescribed in regulations made by the Secretary of State and the Assembly jointly have been complied with in relation to each of the employees of CAFCASS to be transferred under the scheme [s.43(7)].

NB. In s.43 'CAFCASS' has the same meaning as in s. 35.

PART 5

MISCELLANEOUS

Private Fostering

Amendments to Notification Scheme [s.44]

■ The law on private fostering arrangements and the role of local authorities is set out in Part 9 and Schedule 8 of the Children Act 1989 and further detailed in the Children (Private Arrangements for Fostering) Regulations 1991.

■ S. 67 Children Act 1989 (welfare of privately fostered children) is amended by s.44 Children Act 2004 so as to extend the duties of local authorities in cases where the child is proposed to be, though is not yet privately fostered, e.g. the amendments:

- Extend the duty of the local authority to satisfy itself that the welfare of privately fostered children is being satisfactorily safeguarded and promoted so that this duty also applies in respect of those who are proposed to be privately fostered
- Extends the duty to offer advice to private foster carers to include prospective foster carers and/or parents

■ S.44 gives the Secretary of State powers to make regulations about visits by a local authority to privately fostered children and imposing requirements to be met in carrying out its duties under s.67 Children Act 1989.

NB. The intention of such regulations will be to specify what action should be taken when a local authority is notified a child is to be privately fostered so that it can undertake checks, complete assessments and impose requirements or take prohibitive action before a child is fostered.

- The provisions of the Children Act 1989 are amended to confirm that visits are to be completed to premises where it is proposed that a child be privately fostered, not just when s/he has arrived.

- The Secretary of State is also empowered by s.67(6) inserted by s.44(6) to introduce regulations requiring local authorities to monitor discharge of functions under Part 9 Children Act 1989 e.g. record of notifications, compliance with time-scales, prohibitions for collation in an annual report to the LSCB.

NB. In Wales new regulation–making powers will be exercised by the National Assembly for Wales [s.44 (8)].

- S.44 (7) inserts a new para.7A into Schedule 8 Children Act 1989 and will require local authorities to raise public awareness of the requirements to notify the local authority of an intention to privately foster.

Power to Establish Registration Schemes: England and Wales [ss.45 – 47]

■ S.45 in England and s.46 in Wales conferred powers on the Secretary of State and the National Assembly for Wales respectively to set up through regulations, a scheme for the registration of private foster carers.

■ The above central powers were to be exercised only if the (enhanced) local duties and powers proved inadequate and s.47 meant that if no regulations had been made in the relevant country within 4 years of Royal Assent i.e. before 15.11.08 the power to do so would have ceased to have effect.

NB. S.35 Children & Young Persons Act 2008 amended the above provisions so that England and Wales now have until November 2011 to decide whether a registration scheme is necessary in their respective countries.

Child Minding and Day Care

Child Minding and Day Care [s.48]

- S.48 gives effect to Schedule 4 which makes minor amendment to Schedule 9A Children Act 1989 introduced by the Care Standards Act 2000.

Local Authority Services

Payments to Foster Parents [s.49 as amended by Sch.1 Para. 17 Children & Young Persons Act 2008]

■ The appropriate person (Secretary of State with respect to England; National Assembly with respect to Wales [s.49(2)]) may by order make provision as to the payments to be made by:

- A children's services authority in England or Wales or a person exercising functions on its behalf to a local authority foster parent with whom any child is placed by that authority or person under s.22C Children Act 1989
- A voluntary organisation to any person with whom any child is placed by that organisation under s.59(1)(a) Children Act 1989 [s.49(1)]

NB. s.66(4) provides that the first order by the Secretary of State making provisions for payments to foster carers must be approved by resolution of both Houses of Parliament.

Local authority foster parent and voluntary organisation have the same meanings as in the Children Act 1989[s.49 (2)].

Intervention [s.50 as amended by s.194(6) Apprenticeships, Skills, Children and Learning Act 2009]

■ S.497A Education Act 1996 (power to secure proper performance of a local education authority's functions) is to apply to the relevant functions of a children's services authority in England and Wales [s.50(1)]

■ For the purposes of s.50, the relevant functions are those:

- Conferred on or exercisable by the authority which are social services functions, so far as those functions relate to children
- Conferred on the authority under ss.23C to 24D Children Act 1989 (so far as not falling within the above para.)
- Conferred on the authority under ss.10, 12 and s.12C, s.12D and s.17A Children Act 2004 (in England) and ss.25, 26 and 29 (in Wales) [s.50(2)]

NB. The Secretary of State's power to give a direction under s.497A arises when s/he is satisfied a local authority is failing in any respect to perform any relevant function of a local authority to an adequate standard (or at all). The same test will apply to the power as extended by s.50.

Inspection of Local Education Authorities [s.51]

- S.38 Education Act 1997 (inspection of LEAs) is amended by s.51 to allow OfSTED (in England) and Estyn (in Wales) to review any local education authority function, with the exception in England of those that fall within the Adult Learning Inspectorate remit.

- Estyn (in Wales) will be able to review any local education authority function as well as functions under s.25 (co-operation to improve well-being: Wales) and s.26 (children and young people's plans: Wales), so far as those functions relate to education, training or youth support services.

Duty of Local Authorities to Promote Educational Achievement [s.52]

■ S.22 Children Act 1989 (general duty of local authority in relation to children looked after by them), is amended to extend the duty of a local authority under s.22(3)(a) to safeguard and promote the welfare of a child looked after by them to include in particular a duty to promote the child's educational achievement [s.52(1)].

Ascertaining Children's Wishes [s.53]

■ Ss.17, 21 and 47 Children Act 1989 (provision of services to children, provision of accommodation to children and the local authority's duty to investigate respectively) are amended to require that her/his wishes and feelings are sought and (having regard to her/his age and understanding) given due consideration in each case, to the extent that those wishes and feelings have been ascertained.

Information about Individual Children [s.54]

- S.83 Children Act 1989 (research and returns of information), is amended with the effect that the Secretary of State or the Welsh Assembly can obtain from local authorities and voluntary organisations information that may include details relating to, and even identifying individual children.

Social Services Committees [s.55]

■ S.55 repeals s.2 Local Authority Social Services Act 1970 and associated provisions, and thus removes the requirement for local authorities in England and Wales which do not operate executive arrangements under the Local Government Act 2000, to establish a social services committee.

NB. The creation of Directors of Children's Services means that social services committees and indeed social services departments will no longer exist. s.56 amends Schedule 1 Local Authority Social Services Act 1970 to add to the list of 'social services functions' functions relating to LSCBs.

Other Provisions

Fees Payable to Adoption Review Panel Members [s.57]

■ S.12 Adoption and Children Act 2002 (independent review of determinations), is amended by s.56 to the effect that regulations yet to be made, will provide for the payment of fees to panel members.

NB. This amendment is intended to facilitate the recruitment of members to the panels which will be constituted under s.12 Adoption and Children Act 2002 to review adoption agencies' determinations to turn down applicants.

Reasonable Punishment [s.58]

- In relation to any offence specified in s.58 (2) below, 'battery' of a child cannot be justified on the ground that it constituted reasonable punishment.

  NB. Battery is any unwanted application of force to the body of another and is more often called assault.

- The offences referred to in s.58(1) above are:

  - S. 18 or s.20 Offences against the Person Act 1861 (wounding and causing grievous bodily harm)
  - S. 47 Offences against the Person Act 1861 (assault occasioning actual bodily harm)
  - S.1 Children and Young Persons Act 1933 (cruelty to persons under 16) [s.58(2)]

  NB. A parent who committed any of the above offences with respect to her/his own child would be as liable as if the offence had been committed against an adult or a child for whom s/he had no parental role.

- Nor can battery of a child causing 'actual bodily harm' to her/him be justified in any civil proceedings on the ground that it constituted reasonable punishment [s.58 (3)].

- Thus the defence of reasonable chastisement cannot be used in civil proceedings if the battery/assault caused actual bodily harm.

NB. For the purposes of s.58(3) 'actual bodily harm' has the same meaning as it has for the purposes of s. 47 Offences against the Person Act 1861 [s.58(4)].

Thus, actual bodily harm is relatively low level. It need not be permanent but must be more than merely transient or trifling. Bruising is a common example of actual bodily harm.

- s.1 (7) Children and Young Persons Act 1933 (the right of a parent, teacher or other person having lawful control or charge of a child/young person to administer lawful punishment) is revoked [s.58 (5)].

- The net result of the above provisions is that the long established defence of 'reasonable chastisement' is still available for what is technically a 'common assault' on a child by a parent or person with parental authority but not for anything more substantial.

- In January 2010 Sir Roger Singleton (Chief Adviser on the Safety of Children) was asked by the then Secretary of State for his initial views and subsequently an independent report on how the law concerning the defence of 'reasonable punishment' was operating.

- Sir Roger's report was published in March 2010 and recommended that 'the current ban on physical punishment in schools and other children's settings should be extended to include any form of advice, guidance, teaching, training, instruction, worship, treatment or therapy and to any form of care or supervision which is carried out other than by a parent or member of the child's own family or household'.

■ On 30.03.10 the government announced its acceptance of Sir Roger's recommendations and its intention to introduce the required changes to regulation and guidance.

Power to Give Financial Assistance [s.59]

- S.59 amends s.14 Education Act 2002 (power of Secretary of State and Assembly to give financial assistance for purposes related to education or childcare) to give the Secretary of State (in England) and National Assembly (in Wales) the powers to give or make arrangements for the giving of financial assistance.

- The purpose of these powers is the promotion of the welfare of children (defined as under 20s for this purpose) and their parents and the provision of support for parenting.

Child Safety Orders [s.60]

■ S.60 extends the existing circumstances in s.8 Crime and Disorder Act 1998 in which courts can make a Parenting Order and amends the powers to make Child Safety Orders contained in ss.11–13 of that Act.

■ The possibility of a Care Order being made in response to a breach of a Child Safety Order is removed and replaced by the possibility of the making of a Parenting Order.

■ The maximum period for which a Child Safety Order may be made is increased from 3 to 12 months.

Children's Commissioner for Wales: Powers of Entry [s.61]

- S.76 Care Standards Act 2000 (further functions of Children's Commissioner for Wales) is amended.

- The new s.76(8) Care Standards Act 2000 states that:

  - The Commissioner or a person authorised by her/him may for purposes of any function of the Commissioner under s.72B, s.72C or s.72(4) at any reasonable time enter any premises, other than a private dwelling for the purposes of interviewing any child accommodated or living there and, if s/he consents, interview her/him in private

Other Provisions [s.62- 69]

■ The remainder of Part 5 introduces amendments to:

- S.97 Children Act 1989 to clarify that the publication of material from Family Proceedings intended or likely to identify any child as being involved in such proceedings (or her/his address or school) is only prohibited in relation to publication of information to the public or any section of the public.

NB. Rules of court will set out in which circumstances publication may be authorised.

- Schedule 5 Tax Credits Act 2002 to enable the Inland Revenue to share tax credit, child benefit or guardians' allowance information with local authorities for the purposes of enquiries and investigations relating to the welfare of a child under [s.63]

PART 6

GENERAL

- Part 6 sets out:

  - The enactments (listed in Schedule 5) repealed by the Children Act 2004 [s.64]
  - Interpretations of terms (provided at relevant points of the text of this guide) [s.65]
  - The arrangements for regulations and orders which may be made under this Act [s.66]
  - Arrangements for commencement of various provisions of the Act [s.67]

Appendix 1: CAE Publications

From CAE Ltd Pantiles Langham Road Robertsbridge East Sussex TN32 5EP tel: 01580 880243 email: *childact@ dial.pipex.com* or order via our secure on-line facility at *www.caeuk.org*

- Children Act 1989 in The Context of Human Rights Act 1998
- Children Act 2004
- Child Protection
- Residential Care of Children
- 'How Old Do I Have To Be?' (a simple guide to the rights and responsibilities of 0–21 year olds)
- Sexual Offences Act 2003
- Children & Young Persons Act 2008
- Safeguarding Vulnerable Groups Act 2006
- Assessment of Special Educational Needs
- ContactPoint
- Criminal Justice & Immigration Act 2008
- Mental Capacity Act 2005

From CAE Scotland 105 Bishops Park Mid Calder West Lothian EH53 0SR tel: 01506 883885 email *childactScotland@dsl.pipex.com*

- The Children (Scotland) Act 1995 in The Context of the Human Rights Act 1998

www.caeuk.org
Discounts on orders of 50 or more of any one title